# is it Magic?

Rabén & Sjögren  Stockholm

Translation copyright © 1990 by Rabén & Sjögren
All rights reserved
Illustrations copyright © 1986 by Eva Eriksson
Originally published in Sweden by Rabén & Sjögren under the title *Trolleri — Vafalls?*
Text copyright © 1986 by Rose and Samuel Lagercrantz
Library of Congress catalog card number: 89-063054
Printed in Denmark
First edition, 1990

ISBN 91 29 59182 1

R & S Books are distributed in the United States of America
by Farrar, Straus and Giroux, New York;
in the United Kingdom by Ragged Bears, Andover;
in Canada by Vanwell Publishing, St. Catharines
and in Australia by ERA Publications, Adelaide

# Is It Magic?

Rose and Samuel Lagercrantz
Pictures by Eva Eriksson

Translated by Paul Norlen

R&S
BOOKS

Stockholm    New York    Toronto    London    Adelaide

This is a story about a boy, brave little Pete is his name.
He goes to preschool in his town and likes to play this game.
Pete and his best friend, Cilla, pretend to get married each day.
They always start with a fight to get things under way.

And end up building a place to live, a tent or a cabin or house.
Together they run wild around the room . . .

or sit quiet as a mouse.

But one day Billie L., who always acts so tough,
gave our Pete a shove. He was really very rough.
He said, "Hey, little creep! Get out of here. Just go!
Now *I'll* marry Cilla!" And — can you imagine — she didn't say no!

Cilla married Billie L. (How could she have been so mean?)
Little Pete turned as pale as chalk, and then he turned quite green.
He had the blues, and his face got as red as strawberry cake.
He knew he'd never be happy. He knew his heart would break.

On his way home that day, he said, "I need some magic powers!"
And then he didn't say another word for what seemed like several hours.
Although when the Karlson sisters and their little dog passed by,
Pete remembered his manners and mumbled quietly, "Hi."

But it was Mrs. Hellman's cat that really made him think.
Everyone knows that cat is bewitched and it's as black as ink.
It shows up in the strangest places. You never know from where.
It seems to have a sense of when there's magic in the air.
Pete asked it what to do. "Meow" was the only answer he got.

His brother couldn't tell him any more — he had just been given a shot.
Dad had gotten some bills in the mail. Mom had corns on her feet.
And Pete's sister's bicycle had a flat, so she wasn't particularly sweet.
They all had problems of their own and barely listened when he spoke:
"Can't you give me any help? Do you think this is a joke?"

What did they finally give him? A magic wand (which looked all right),
an old hat, and a special book.

And, by then, day had turned to night.

Mom slept like an oak-tree, and Dad slept like a stick in repose.
Pete's brother slept more like a branch . . .

and his sister slept curled like a rose.

But Pete couldn't sleep that night. His mind was on one track.
His book was called *Is It Magic?* and he read it from front to back.
The book described what you should do if you get so furious
you want to scare someone. (Now, aren't you a bit curious?)
HOW TO TURN INTO A LION …

Bathe in pancake batter until you are almost gold.
Do not wash the batter off until the weather's cold.
Take sixteen steps around the house, and howl, so everyone hears.
The sound should be heard throughout the town by anything with ears.

To become a giraffe, you must close your eyes for a hundred and eighty-nine days,
and stretch your neck so that it's long and in the treetops sways.
Seen from above, the people who shove are only pinpricks, really small.
Once you get a little perspective, some things don't seem important at all.
But if you want to be a snake, you have to do more than hiss.
Get yourself a snake costume, then do exactly this:
First you creep, then you crawl, and here's where you get the feel!
If you never stand up straight again, you've become a snake for real.

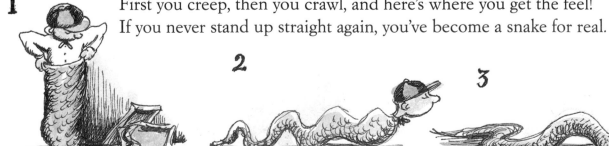  

Or do you want to be a camel, solemn and slender but tough?
Then walk backward around Africa. One circuit will be enough.
The book notes, later on, that changing to a bull would take one hour.
Another page tells you what to do to become a dinosaur.
Press your chin to the ground, and leave it for thirty days plus one,
while you mumble the well-known words "Hocus pocus." Then you're done.

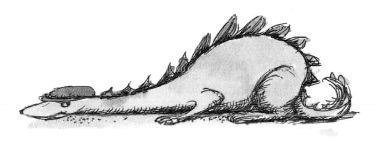

On page 93 you can read about weird birds like the king's bassoon.
Turn yourself into one of those, or maybe a tripe-snipe, or an asphalt loon.
Or think about being a rubbish wren, or an icicle-crested peewit.
Or a notch-eagle, or a lamp-plover, or a bellowing flagpole egret.

Pete read the book all night. There were things he had to know.
He read while he was dressing himself, and then it was time to go.

He read when he got to school. He couldn't sit still in his chair.
And finally he decided to turn himself into a bear.
But that wasn't easy, because the children came over to see,
even though he told them firmly, "Go away! You're disturbing me!"
Everyone thought he could do it, but Billie L. disagreed,
although he himself was dying to become a coal-black steed . . .

Pete looked through the book and on page 5 found his source.
"It's very easy! Go to sleep and then you'll turn into a horse.
Listen to what I say. Lie down. That's all you have to do.
Keep your eyes closed while I sing a lullaby to you."
And he began to sing, "Abracadabra, dabra fleece,
abracadabra, little Billie, sleep, dear one, in peace!"

When Billie had fallen asleep, little Pete said, "It's my turn today.
Get a veil, Cilla, come on! Get some flowers and let's play!"

But — nothing happened. Not a single thing.
Cilla didn't want to play; she didn't want a ring.
Cilla wanted to be enchanted; she wanted to be a crocodile.
And Harold wanted to be a panther, and run for many a mile.
Anna wanted to be a shark, and her little brother Tye
wanted to be something, too, like a dragon, towering high!
Samuel wanted to be a wasp, to buzz and sting and whirl.
Jenny wanted to have stripes and turn into a zebra girl.
Daniel wanted to be a worm and Nora to be an auk,
Maria a bright blue butterfly, and Victoria a soaring hawk.

They all shouted at once, "It's my turn now!"
Until finally Pete read, "This is how to turn into a kangaroo —
eat nothing at all."
They shrieked so loud you could hear the noise
way down the hall.

And so not one of them would eat the hot rose-hip soup.
"Please explain! Have you lost your minds?" Miss Sue said to the group.
But Pete crept out of the room (so he could hide under his hat),
and very softly, he said, "I think I'll turn into a cat."

Suddenly there was a lot of confusion. A cat hopped right up
onto the table where they were sitting, knocking over a cup.
Miss Maud couldn't keep from laughing, Miss Annette was shaken,
and Miss Sue was so worked up that Billie L. awakened.

"Out," she shrieked, hysterical. "Cats are the one thing I can't stand!"
She chased it round the room. The situation was out of hand.
But Cilla shouted, "Pete, turn yourself back, please do.
If you'll only be yourself again, I promise to marry you."

Poor Cilla cried and cried. She didn't comprehend
that she had kissed Mrs. Hellman's cat, and not her very best friend.
Now, if anything in this story truly has a magic cast
it is perhaps the fact that this cat happened to come walking past,
and then, zip zoom! was gone again . . .

                                          But it wasn't long before

Pete was waving his magic wand and standing by the door,
saying, "Wow! I'm very hungry! When can we get some chow?"

But all the children, wanting to be cats, had started to meow.
Then Miss Maud said, "Now it's your turn to go marry Cilla, Pete."

And so they've been having weddings every single week.
But what about Pete? Is there anything more to say?
Well, time will pass and Pete will be a man one day . . .

He'll enchant his wife and his children, too.
Magic's something you must try your whole life through.